LIFESAVERS!
STORIES AND SKILLS

Steve Bunnell

illustrated by Nicholas P. Soloway

Cover Photograph © 1992 by Sharon Cummings / DEMBINSKY PHOTO ASSOC.

1 2 3 4 5 6 7 8 9 10

ISBN 0-8251-2391-7

Copyright © 1993

J. Weston Walch, Publisher

P.O. Box 658 • Portland, Maine 04104-0658

Printed in the United States of America

Contents

To the Reader v

PART I. At Home

1. Night Fire 3
Escaping a home fire at night

2. The Baby-Sitter 9
Child poisoning emergency

3. Mr. Fix-It 13
Home electrical hazards

4. The Caller 17
Handling unwanted callers

5. Close Call in the Kitchen 23
Handling a kitchen fire

PART II. In the Neighborhood

6. Street Smarts 31
Practicing street safety

7. In the Big City 37
How to avoid being robbed

8. Sam's Last Delivery 41
Helping an unconscious person

9. The School Trip 47
Being lost in the city

PART III. On the Road

10. Joy Ride 53
Driving safety

11. Jack's Dream Date 57
Handling a flat tire

12. Full Throttle 63
Motorcycle do's and don'ts

13. The Mountain Road 69
Winter driving safety

14. Hit and Run 75
Hit-and-run emergency

To the Reader

Things can go wrong. Accidents can happen. But did you know that most accidents can be prevented? Most accidents are caused by carelessness, poor planning, or lack of information. Most accidents don't *have* to happen!

But accidents that didn't have to happen cause more medical problems than all diseases put together.

This book will show you ways to be safer at home, in your neighborhood, and on the road. Some stories will show you how to prevent a bad thing from happening. Other stories will teach you what to do when something does go wrong.

You will learn how to avoid or handle fourteen different kinds of emergencies. After you read the stories and practice the activities, you will know such life-saving things as:

- how to handle a kitchen fire
- how to lessen your chances of being robbed on the street
- how to keep from skidding off an icy road.

Have fun with the stories and skill activities. Then have a safer and happier life!

PART I. At Home

Night Fire

EMERGENCY #1

Dan woke up in the middle of the night and smelled smoke. Something was wrong!

Dan got out of bed. He rushed to his closed bedroom door. Even though the doorknob felt warm, he pulled the door open.

A blast of smoke and fire nearly knocked him over. He fought frantically to get the door closed again. This was a real fire!

With his room full of smoke, Dan coughed as he felt his way to the window. The smoke was so thick he couldn't see a thing.

In the dark, he couldn't remember how to unlatch the window. He picked up his desk chair and smashed the window. Glass shattered everywhere.

Then Dan pushed himself through the jagged glass and crawled out on the second-story roof. It was a long way to the ground! But with nowhere else to go, he just closed his eyes and jumped.

Dazed and in shock, Dan wandered into the front yard. He met up with his mother, father, and older brother. Dan was bleeding from cuts all over his body. He discovered later that he also had a sprained ankle and a broken arm.

The family was happy they had all managed to escape. Their dog, Lucky, had not been so fortunate.

Dan's brother had tried to go back into the house to save the dog. But the smoke was too thick and the flames were too hot. The house was destroyed and Lucky was killed by the fire.

(Fire investigators later discovered the cause of the fire. It had been started by Christmas tree lights that were left on during the night. They also discovered that the batteries in all the smoke alarms had not been replaced in two years. There were no fire extinguishers in the house.)

NIGHT FIRE

Activity Sheet 1

QUESTIONS TO TALK ABOUT

1. What actions could Dan and his family have taken *to prevent* this emergency?

2. What mistakes did Dan make during the actual emergency? What should he have done *to handle* the emergency differently?

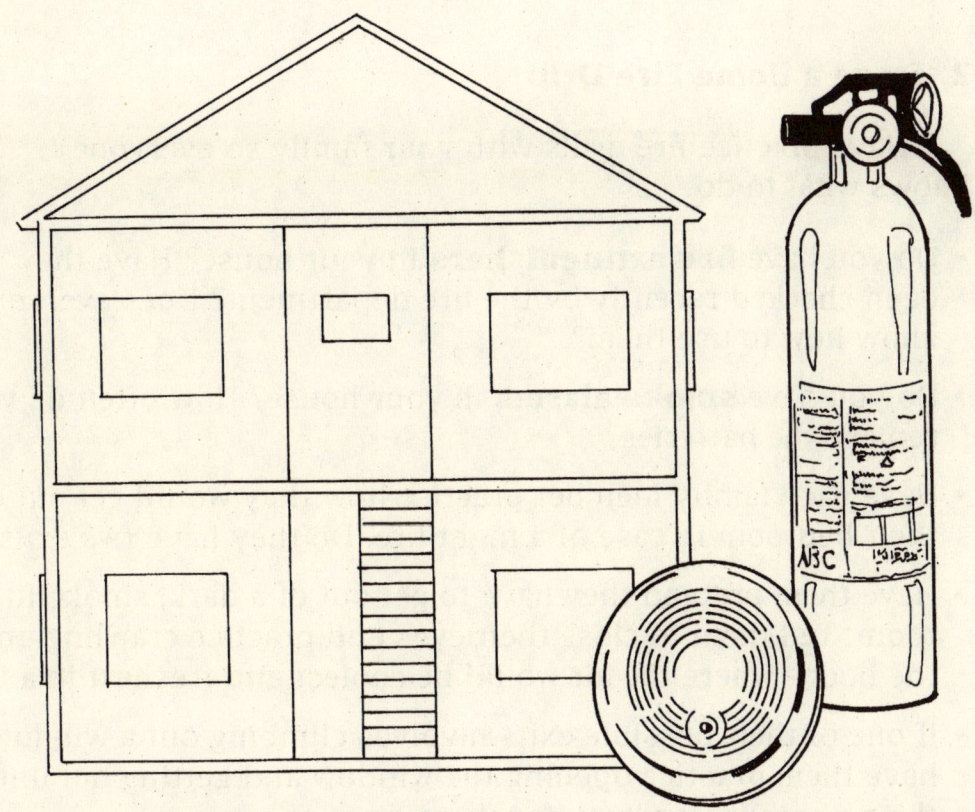

Activities to Try

1. Plan Two Fire Escape Routes for Every Person in Your House

In case of fire, there should be *two* possible exits from every room in your house.

Draw a map of where each person in your house sleeps at night. With a *red* pen or crayon, draw an arrow to show the easiest exit (the central hallway, for example).

With a *blue* pen or crayon, draw an arrow to show a second possible exit (such as a window).

Does each person have *two* available exits? If not, could another exit be made available? (For example, by opening an adjoining door?)

2. Stage a Home Fire Drill

Have practice fire drills with your family so everyone knows what to do.

- Do you have **fire extinguishers** in your house? Have they been checked recently by the fire department? Does everyone know how to use them?

- Do you have **smoke alarms** in your house? How often do you replace the batteries?

- Have each family member practice how they would get out of their bedroom in case of a night fire. Do they have *two* exits?

- Have them pretend they have to get out of a dark, smoke-filled room. Tell them to close their eyes and practice crawling on the floor—where the air would be coolest and freshest in a fire.

- If one of their possible exits involves climbing out a window, have them practice opening the window and getting out until the process is *very* easy for them.

- Remind everyone *not* to open a door if it is warm to the touch or if smoke is visible around the edges.

    To keep smoke from coming in the room, they should put a piece of towel or piece of clothing on the floor to block the space under the door.

- Ask your local fire department for more information on fire prevention and home fires.

The Baby-Sitter

EMERGENCY #2

Cheryl had been been baby-sitting for the Williams family all summer. It was her first summer working as a baby-sitter.

The Williams children liked Cheryl a lot. Michael was two years old and Sarah was four. They were quite active. Sometimes Cheryl got very tired taking care of them.

One hot afternoon, Michael and Sarah were taking their afternoon naps. Cheryl was feeling a little lonely.

She decided to call her boyfriend, Tom. Talking to Tom always made her feel better.

Cheryl must have lost track of the time. Suddenly she heard a noise. It was little Michael's voice down in the basement.

Cheryl rushed into the hallway. The children's bedroom door was wide open. The door to the basement was open, too. Cheryl raced downstairs.

There was Michael, drinking from a large plastic bottle of laundry detergent! She grabbed him and ran upstairs.

Michael started to cry very loudly. "I want my Mommy!" he wailed.

Cheryl panicked. She didn't know what to do. She didn't have a telephone number to reach the children's parents.

Sarah woke up and ran in from the bedroom. When she saw Michael crying, she started crying, too.

Cheryl had never felt so frightened in her life. Her mind was a total blank. She couldn't think of one single thing to do to handle the emergency!

At that moment, the phone rang. It was Mrs. Carter, a neighbor from next door, who wanted to sell a raffle ticket to Mrs. Williams.

Cheryl overcame her panic and told Mrs. Carter about Michael drinking the laundry detergent. Mrs. Carter told Cheryl not to worry and said she'd be right over to help.

Cheryl counted every second until Mrs. Carter arrived.

THE BABY-SITTER

Activity Sheet 2

QUESTIONS TO TALK ABOUT

1. What actions should Cheryl have taken *to prevent* this emergency?

2. What mistakes did Cheryl make in handling the actual emergency? What could she have done *to handle* the emergency differently?

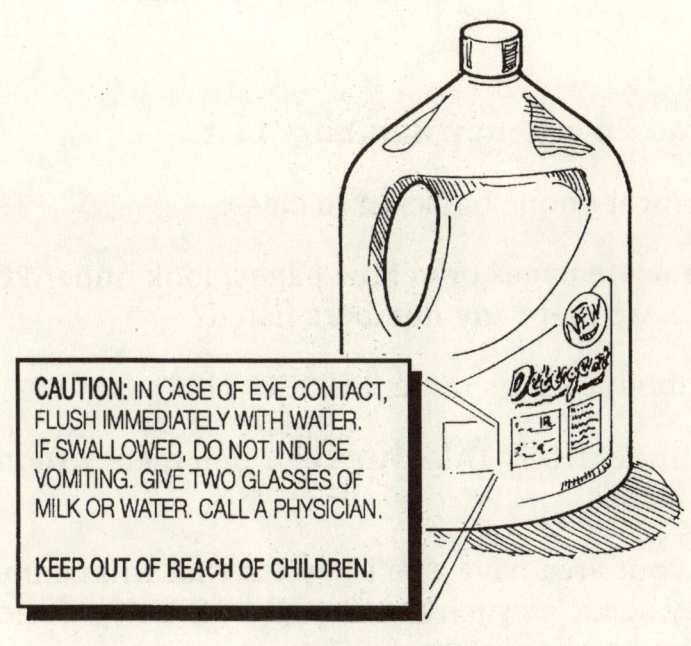

POISON –
POLICE –
FIRE –
HOSPITAL –
RESCUE –

Activities to Try

1. Study Labels for Poison Emergency Information

Bring in from home as many different empty bottles of household liquids and powders as you can find. Include items such as detergents, bleaches, and cleansers.

Read the labels on each product. Do the labels tell what to do if someone drinks or eats the product?

Compare the different advice given on each label. (For example, do some tell you to give the victim milk? water? nothing to drink at all?)

After reading the labels, would *you* know what to do if you found that a child had swallowed the product?

2. Make an Emergency Numbers List

Bring local phone books in to class.

In the white pages or yellow pages, look under POISON CONTROL. Are there any numbers listed?

How about listings under POLICE? FIRE?

Look under HOSPITALS. Are their emergency room numbers listed?

Does your area have a 911 system that will connect you to emergency agencies such as the police, fire department, hospital, and rescue service?

With the help of your teacher, make a list of the best emergency numbers for your area. Make a copy of this list for your family. Put it up in an important place by a phone in your home. Take another copy to your baby-sitting jobs.

Mr. Fix-It

EMERGENCY #3

Jerry is a teenager who brags about being able to fix *anything*! He is always taking apart things like toasters, televisions, and tape players to "repair" them.

The truth is, however, that Jerry doesn't know as much about fixing things as he thinks. He is also very impatient. He rarely takes the time to give his repair jobs the care they really require.

Jerry's mother had inherited a valuable, antique lamp that needed to be rewired. She was going to take it to the repair shop. But Jerry insisted, "Let me take care of it, Mom. I can fix it in no time."

When Jerry's mother went out, he started to work on the lamp. His father had given him a book on electrical repair, but Jerry decided he didn't need to read it.

After he rewired the lamp, Jerry plugged it in to see what would happen. There was a flash. Then the room went completely dark. The electricity for the whole room was out.

Untroubled, Jerry went down into the cellar where the fuse box was. He couldn't find a new fuse to replace the old one.

Then he remembered a trick he had heard about. Jerry took a penny from his pocket and stuck it in the fuse box. "That'll take care of it," he said.

Jerry went back upstairs and plugged in the lamp again. This time the electricity did not go out.

But suddenly the room was filled with sparks and smoke. There was no way he could unplug the lamp because it was sparking so much.

By the time the fire department arrived, the room—along with Jerry's mother's antique lamp—had been completely destroyed in the electrical fire.

MR. FIX-IT

Activity Sheet 3

QUESTIONS TO TALK ABOUT

1. What actions could Jerry have taken *to prevent* this emergency?

2. What should Jerry have done *to handle* this emergency situation differently?

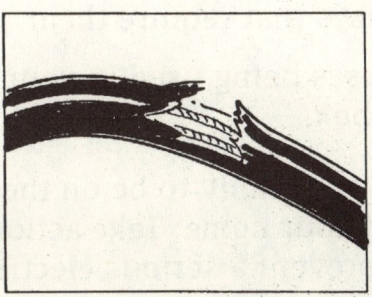
Frayed cord

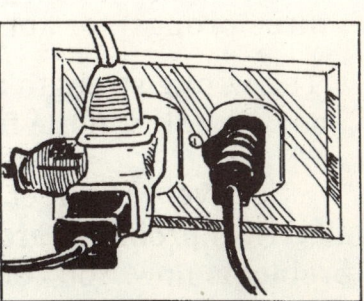
Overloaded outlets

Cords under rug

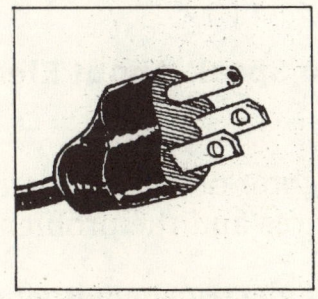
3-Prong plug

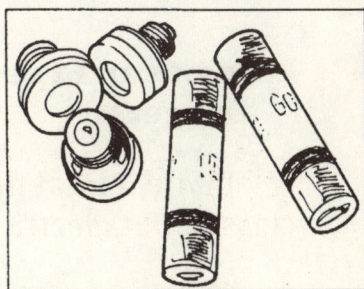
Fuses

Activities to Try

1. Checklist for Looking for Causes of an Electrical Fire

Many electrical fires can be prevented by looking for possible problems around your home.

Can you spot any of these problems in your house?

- Brittle or frayed cords on lamps, radios, TV's, etc.
- Overloaded electrical outlets—too many appliances or extension cords plugged into one wall outlet
- Electrical cords—or extension cords—that run under a rug
- Not using properly grounded outlets or extension cords (with three prongs) for appliances that require them
- The wrong strength in fuses being used in your electrical fuse box, or coins in the fuse box.

Get every member of your family to be on the lookout for electrical problems around your home. Take action to fix those problems now. You could prevent a serious electrical emergency.

2. Invite an Expert to Speak About Electrical Dangers

Invite a local firefighter or an electrician to talk to your class about electrical fires and the problems that cause them.

Think about Jerry's electrical emergency.

- What more can you learn about *preventing* electrical fires?
- What can you learn about *fighting* an electrical fire?

The Caller

EMERGENCY #4

Debbie's older brother and sister went out to a movie with their parents. But Debbie stayed home to work on a science fair project.

Just as she had gotten down to work, the phone rang. Debbie picked up the receiver. "Hello?" she said.

"Hello," said a man's voice in an odd whisper. Debbie didn't recognize the caller's voice.

"Hello?" she repeated, a little nervously.

"Are your parents home?" the man asked with a strange laugh.

"No," Debbie said.

There was a pause on the other end of the line.

"Is anyone else there?" the voice finally asked.

"No!" Debbie responded firmly. She was really beginning to get anxious.

There was another pause.

"Well, what's *your* name?" the voice asked, quietly.

Debbie began to get very suspicious. Quickly she hung up the phone.

Thirty seconds later, it rang again. Hoping it was someone she knew, Debbie picked it up.

"Hello again, my little friend," said the strange man's voice. "Why did you hang up on me? Don't you want to talk?"

Then he laughed softly.

"Leave me alone!" cried Debbie, almost bursting into tears.

The voice laughed quietly again. "I thought you'd be lonely with no one else around."

"Just leave me alone!" Debbie said again. She slammed down the phone this time.

Thirty seconds later, the phone rang for the third time. Debbie didn't answer it. It just kept ringing and ringing.

Finally she couldn't take it anymore. She spotted her father's coaching whistle on the dinner table. She rushed over and put the whistle to her lips.

Running back to the phone, she picked up the receiver. Then Debbie blew the whistle into the phone as loudly as she could, and hung up.

Afterwards, Debbie sat perfectly still. Then she began to tremble all over and burst into tears.

THE CALLER

Activity Sheet 4

QUESTIONS TO TALK ABOUT

1. What actions could Debbie have taken *to prevent* this emergency?

2. What mistakes did Debbie make in how she dealt with the caller? What could she have done *to handle* the emergency differently?

Activities to Try

1. Talk About Disturbing Phone Experiences That You Have Had

Have *you* ever had to deal with a problem phone call such as the following?

- A pushy salesperson?
- A "crank" call from someone playing a trick?
- An abusive or obscene call from a disturbed person?

Share your experience with others in your class. Tell what happened. How did the call make you feel?

How did you handle the situation? Would you do anything differently if you had to handle the call today?

2. Practice Handling Difficult Calls

One way to get better at handling difficult phone calls is to practice by role-playing calls with your classmates.

1. First, practice acting out a phone call from a pushy telephone salesperson. The student who plays the SALESPERSON should do everything possible to try to get information out of the VICTIM. (For example: his or her name; information about the family, etc.) The SALESPERSON should also try to do everything to keep the VICTIM from hanging up.

VICTIMS should try to avoid being tricked into giving out any personal information about themselves, their families, or their neighbors. They should find a way to politely end the conversation.

2. With your classmates, take turns role-playing the parts of ANNOYER and VICTIM in an annoyance call, such as Debbie had to handle. The ANNOYER should try to do everything possible to make the VICTIM show anger or fear.

The VICTIM should try *not* to express any feelings such as anger at the caller. The VICTIM also should *not* try to get "revenge" by blowing a whistle or yelling into the phone. The VICTIM should end the conversation calmly and quickly.

Close Call in the Kitchen

EMERGENCY #5

Sally's aunt was going to be away for the day. She asked Sally to watch her young cousins, Jeffrey and Jane.

In the afternoon Jeffrey and Jane wanted a snack. They asked Sally to make popcorn for them. They loved to hear the sound of it popping in the pot.

Sally started heating oil in a large pot on the top of the stove. The kids went into the other room to draw while they waited.

Just as the oil started to get hot, the phone rang in the kitchen. At the same time, five-year-old Jeffrey came running in. He wanted to show Sally the picture he had just drawn.

As Sally was trying to take the pot with the oil off the hot burner, Jeffrey bumped Sally's arm. The oil spilled all over the stove top.

With a whoosh, the whole top of the stove was in flames!

Jeffrey began to cry. Sally didn't know what to do.

"Where's the fire extinguisher, Jeffrey?" she yelled. He was too scared to answer.

She grabbed a dishtowel and tried to put out the flames. But the dishtowel caught fire, too!

Then Sally searched for something in the cupboard to throw on the fire.

She grabbed a box of cornstarch and sprinkled it over the fire. But the cornstarch only made the fire burn higher!

Desperate, Sally rushed to the phone extension in the other room. In her panic, she could not remember what number to call for help. It took her a long time to find a phone book because she was trying to comfort the frightened children at the same time.

By the time the fire truck arrived, the kitchen was completely destroyed. Luckily the fire did not spread to other parts of the house.

Sally was not so lucky. In the process of trying to put out the fire, she suffered first-degree burns all over her hands and arms.

CLOSE CALL IN THE KITCHEN

Activity Sheet 5

QUESTIONS TO TALK ABOUT

1. What actions should Sally have taken *to prevent* this emergency?

2. What mistakes did Sally make during the emergency? What should she have done *to handle* the emergency differently?

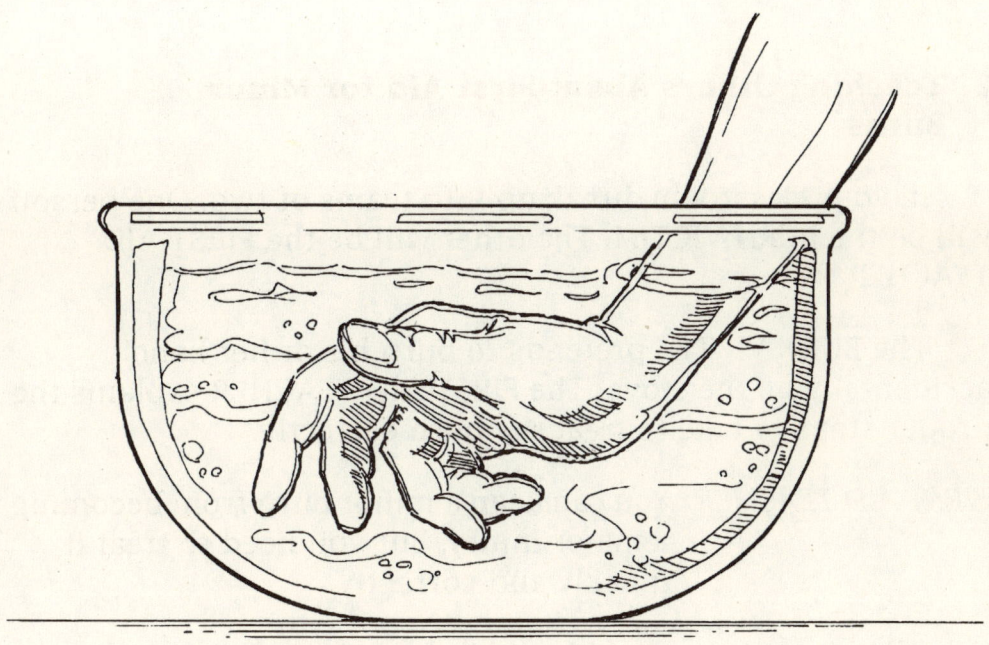

Activities to Try

1. Make Sure You Know How to Call for Fire Help—Fast!

If there were a fire in your house, would *you* know how to call for help the fastest way?

Find out the best fire emergency number for you to call in your area. Ask your parents or teacher to help you.

Then, make sure this number is clearly posted near *every* phone in your home.

Remember, just minutes lost in getting help can make the difference between minor damage or a major loss.

2. Teaching Others About First Aid for Minor Burns

In your classroom, break up into teams of two. One person will be the BURN VICTIM. The other will be the FIRST AID TEACHER.

The BURN VICTIM pretends to burn his or her hand accidentally on the stove. The FIRST AID TEACHER explains the proper steps to take to treat the burn correctly.

FIRST AID TEACHER: You can keep a minor burn from becoming a major injury. But you need to treat it quickly and correctly.

(*VICTIM* acts out burning his or her hand.)

FIRST AID TEACHER: **Step 1**: Put ice on the burn, or put the burned area in very cold water.

(*VICTIM* puts hand in bowl of cold water.)

FIRST AID TEACHER: **Step 2**: Do *not* put grease, butter, or cream on the burn. This keeps the burn "cooking."

(*VICTIM* reaches for some cream, then decides not to use it.)

FIRST AID TEACHER: **Step 3**: Keep the burn area cold in this way for *10 minutes*. The cold is needed to keep down the swelling.

(*VICTIM* keeps hand in bowl of water.)

FIRST AID TEACHER: **Step 4**: If a blister forms after a while, do not break it. This could lead to infection.

(*VICTIM* inspects hand for a blister.)

FIRST AID TEACHER: **Step 5**: If the blister breaks, wash the burn area with soap and water. Then cover with an adhesive bandage.

(*VICTIM* washes burn with soap and water and covers with bandage.)

FIRST AID TEACHER: **Step 6**: If the burn doesn't heal quickly, be sure to see a doctor.

When you have practiced your skit, you can perform it for other classes if you would like to.

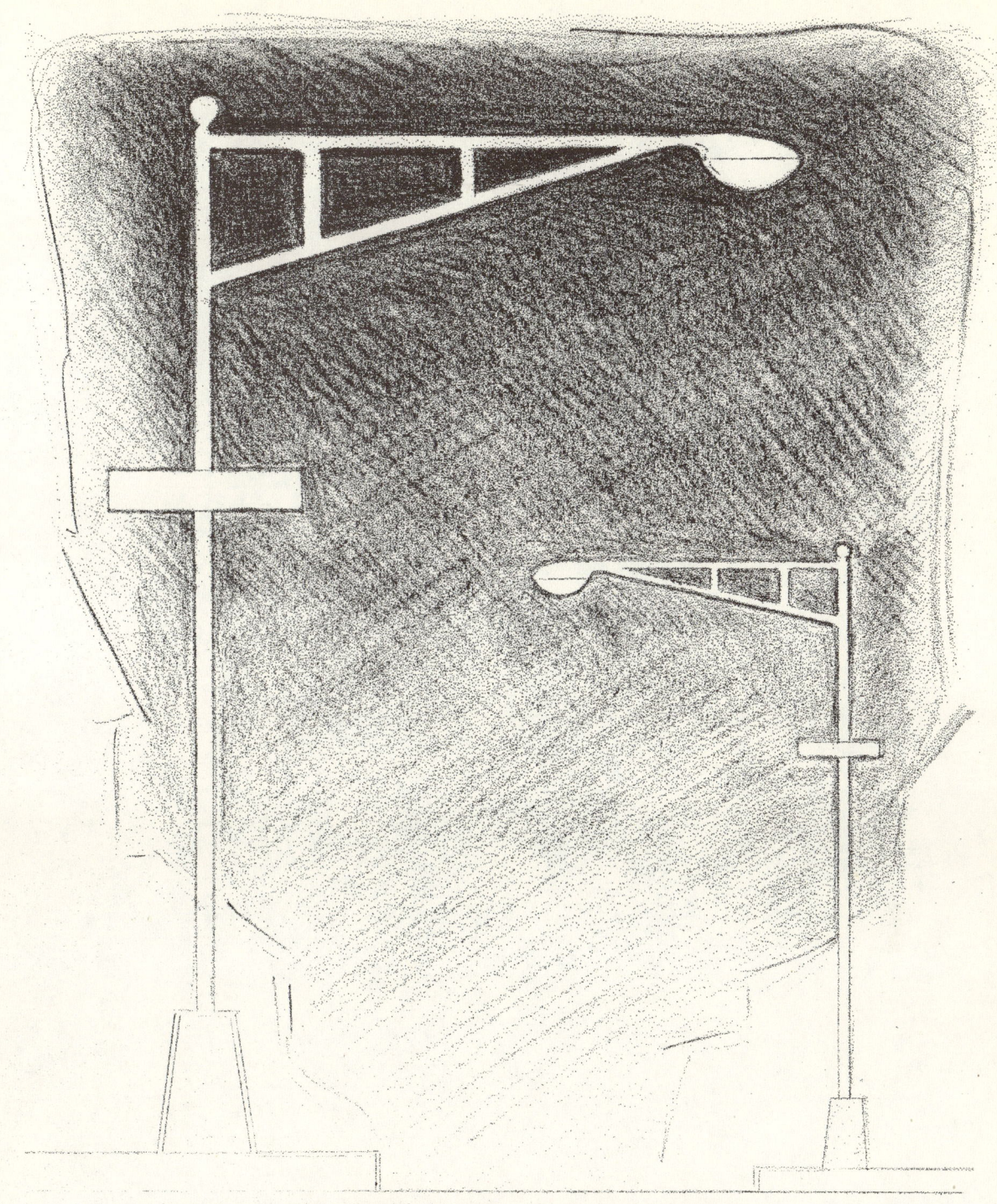

PART II. In the Neighborhood

Street Smarts

EMERGENCY #6

One Saturday night, Gina went to a party with two of her friends.

The party was in a section of town far away from her neighborhood. So one of her girlfriends drove all three of them.

At midnight the party started breaking up. Then Gina discovered that her friends had already left.

Suddenly she realized that she had no ride home.

Gina was upset for a minute. Then she came up with the perfect solution. She would *walk* home—even though it was over three miles to her house!

"Why not?" she reasoned with herself. "It's a nice, warm night."

She said goodbye to everyone and started walking. The streets were quiet. At first the idea seemed like a lot of fun. But a half-mile into her walk, Gina started to get tired.

As she was passing through the downtown area, she got an idea.

"By cutting through the market district, I could cut fifteen minutes off my walk," Gina thought. She decided to take the chance on the shortcut.

The market district was poorly lit. The street lamps were widely separated and the area looked deserted.

All of a sudden, Gina began to feel a little uneasy.

She had the scary feeling that she was not alone. She thought she heard footsteps.

Gina's heart started to race. Her pace quickened. She looked around nervously. But she couldn't see anyone in the gloomy light.

There definitely *were* footsteps behind her. And the footsteps were keeping up with hers as she walked faster and faster.

Gina tried to run. But she couldn't move very fast in her new party shoes.

She tripped. She got up. She ran faster.

She was losing her breath. The person behind her was catching up.

Gina fell again. This time she couldn't get up. She was too tired and scared.

The last thing she remembered was a dark figure standing over her...

STREET SMARTS

Activity Sheet 6

QUESTIONS TO TALK ABOUT

1. What actions could Gina have taken *to prevent* this emergency?

2. What mistakes did Gina make in handling the situation in the market district? What could she have done *to handle* the emergency differently?

Activities to Try

1. Problem Solving—Make Your Own Choice

Pretend you are walking alone at night on a dark street that is unfamiliar to you.

All of a sudden, you feel that you are being followed.

Here are five possible choices for handling the situation:

(1) Keep walking steadily. Don't show that you are scared.
(2) Go up to the front door of a house that looks safe and ring the bell.
(3) Look for an unlocked car on the street. Get in and lock the doors.
(4) Run.
(5) Yell for help.

Which choice do you think is the *best* strategy? Tell why.

Which choice do you think is the *worst* strategy? Tell why.

Have *you*, like Gina, ever actually been followed in an unfamiliar place? Tell what happened. What strategy did you choose to handle it?

2. Making a Safety Map of Your Neighborhood

Draw a map of the "safe" spots in your neighborhood:

- Mark which streets are busiest, even at night.

- Mark any deserted areas (vacant lots, empty houses, etc.) that you should avoid.
- Mark streets that have the brightest street lighting.
- Mark any dark streets or areas you should avoid.
- Mark what stores you would feel safe going into.
- Mark what neighbors' houses you would feel safe going to.
- Mark any other areas that seem safe to you.
- Mark any other areas that seem unsafe to you.

The next time you are walking in your neighborhood, think about what you have learned by drawing this safety map.

In the Big City

EMERGENCY #7

Bill was excited about visiting his Uncle Rob. His uncle lived in the city. It was over 200 miles away from the small town where Bill and his family lived.

On Friday afternoon after school, Bill got on the bus to the city. He arrived at the bus station in the city just as it was getting dark. He was very excited.

Bill got off the bus, carrying his overnight bag. He walked across the busy lobby to buy a can of cola at the newspaper stand.

To pay for the drink, Bill opened up his wallet and took out a $100 bill. He had received the money for his birthday and had saved it as spending money for this trip.

The woman at the newspaper stand seemed angry at having to cash such a large bill. But she found the correct change for him. Bill thanked her and moved on.

A few steps away, a young man stopped Bill and asked him for the time. Bill looked at his watch. It was an expensive gold one that he had inherited from his grandfather. It meant a lot to him.

"7:10," Bill told him. The young man hurried away.

Bill left the bus station and walked along the dark street to call a cab. Suddenly he heard footsteps. He realized he was being followed.

Before he knew it, Bill was surrounded by a gang of three.

"How about handing over that wallet, kid?" one growled.

"Yeah, and how about that nice watch while you're at it?" another hissed.

Bill had been saving that money for a long time. And the watch had belonged to his grandfather. There was no way he was going to give them anything.

"No!" he said angrily, and turned to run.

In an instant they had him on the ground. One grabbed his wallet and watch. Another started kicking him—hard.

It was a good thing that someone came along. The gang ran off, leaving Bill moaning on the ground with six fractured ribs.

IN THE BIG CITY

Activity Sheet 7

QUESTIONS TO TALK ABOUT

1. What actions should Bill have taken *to prevent* this emergency?

2. What mistakes did Bill make in dealing with the thugs? What should he have done *to handle* the emergency differently?

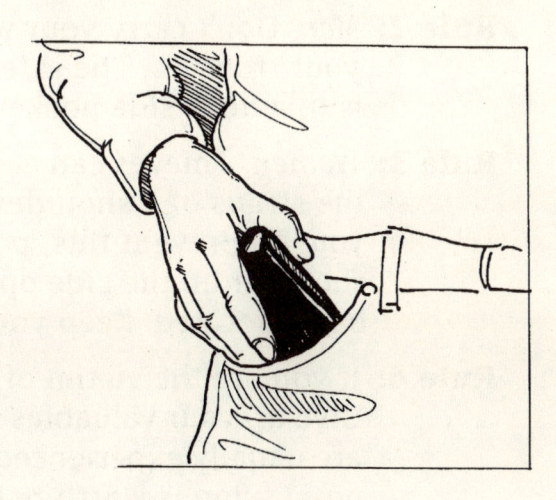

Activities to Try

1. Make Up Skits About How to Avoid Being Robbed

There are some things you *can* do to lessen the chance of being robbed.

Break up into small teams. Make up a short skit about ways to avoid being robbed. Base your skit on one of the rules below—or make up a rule of your own to demonstrate.

Rule 1: Don't display money, watches, or jewelry that might attract the attention of thieves.

Rule 2: *Men:* Don't carry your wallet in the back pocket of your trousers. The safest (pickpocket-proof) place is in a deep side pocket of your trousers.

Rule 3: *Women:* Thieves can easily put their arms through the straps of a shoulder bag and pull it away from you. To prevent this, put the strap over the shoulder on the side opposite from where your bag is located. Keep your hand on the strap.

Rule 4: If you are the victim of a robbery, don't resist. Give up your valuables without a struggle. Thieves are usually experienced and often desperate. *No* possession is worth risking being injured or even killed for!

2. Share Your Story

Have *you* ever been involved in a robbery situation like Bill's? Tell what happened.

How did you handle the situation?

Do you now recognize any ways that you might have been able to *prevent* the situation?

Sam's Last Delivery

EMERGENCY #8

For three afternoons a week, Sam worked for the supermarket in his neighborhood. Part of his job involved making deliveries.

Many of the people on Sam's delivery route were elderly people. They found it hard to get to the store. They always enjoyed talking with Sam when he delivered the groceries.

Mr. Carlson was the last person on Sam's route. He was eighty-five years old and lived alone. Sam liked Mr. Carlson best because he was so friendly and told funny stories.

One day Sam walked up the steps to Mr. Carlson's house and rang the bell. Sam didn't hear anything inside.

This was not like Mr. Carlson. He was usually at the door even before Sam reached the doorbell.

Sam rang the bell again. Still there was no sound. Sam was puzzled, because he could see all the lights on inside.

Sam was getting concerned. He remembered that Mr. Carlson had looked sick last week. When Sam had asked him if he felt okay, Mr. Carlson had just smiled and said, "Don't worry about me, Sam."

Sam tried the door. It was unlocked. He walked inside.

"Mr. Carlson? Mr. Carlson?" he called. No answer.

Sam looked in the living room—no one there. He looked in the kitchen—no one there, either. Sam decided to look upstairs.

Finally, in the bedroom at the top of the stairs, Sam found Mr. Carlson. He was lying unconscious on the rug.

Suddenly Sam felt very frightened. He had never faced an emergency like this. He had no idea what to do!

Sam bent down to wake Mr. Carlson up. He shook Mr. Carlson's body very hard. But Mr. Carlson did not wake up.

Sam went into the bathroom. He filled a glass with water and poured it over Mr. Carlson's face. Again there was no response.

Remembering something he had seen on television, Sam bent down and blew into Mr. Carlson's mouth. Still nothing happened.

Sam didn't know what else to try. He was really scared. So Sam ran down the stairs and out the door, leaving Mr. Carlson just as he found him.

When Sam arrived back at the supermarket, he told his boss about finding Mr. Carlson. Within minutes, an ambulance was on its way.

SAM'S LAST DELIVERY

Activity Sheet 8

QUESTIONS TO TALK ABOUT

1. Could Sam have taken any actions that might have helped *to prevent* this emergency?

2. What mistakes did Sam make when he found Mr. Carlson unconscious? What should Sam have done *to handle* the emergency differently?

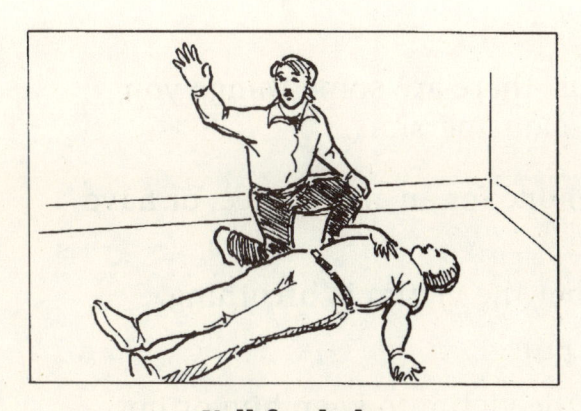

Yell for help

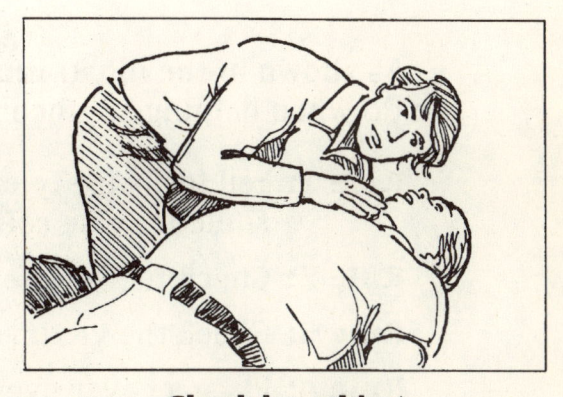

Check breathing

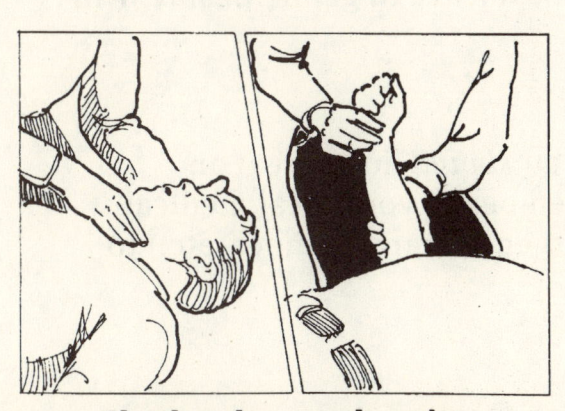

Check pulse—neck, wrist

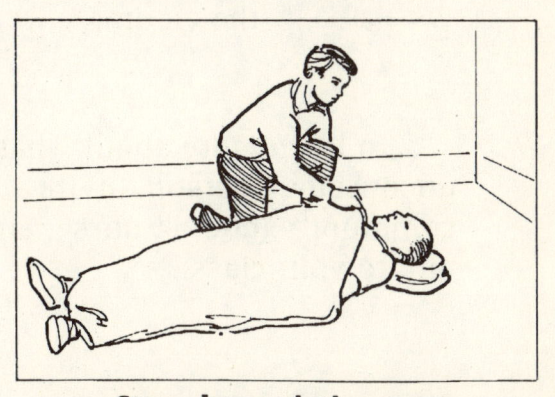

Stay—keep victim warm

Activities to Try

1. First Aid: Helping an Unconscious Person

There are many things you should *not* do when helping an unconscious person. Here are a few rules:

Rule 1: *Don't* pour water on the victim's face or try to get the person to drink liquids. (The liquid could block air passages.)

Rule 2: *Don't* try to move the victim—especially if you suspect broken bones or other internal injuries.

Rule 3: *Don't* try to give the victim mouth-to-mouth resuscitation unless you have been trained to do so.

Rule 4: *Don't* leave the victim until help arrives.

As shown in the illustrations, there are some things you *can* do when helping an unconscious person:

Rule 1: Yell for help. Telephone for an ambulance, or have someone else call.

Rule 2: Check to see whether the victim is breathing.

Rule 3: Check the victim's pulse.

Rule 4: Place a cover over the victim to keep him or her warm. Unless you *must* leave to get help, stay with the victim.

To learn more about what you *should* do to treat an unconscious person, invite a member of your local medical community (doctor, nurse, emergency team member, etc.) to talk to your class.

2. Learning to Read Pulses

Your pulse rate is the number of times your heart beats in one minute. A pulse rate that is far above or far below the normal rate can indicate a serious problem.

The average normal pulse rate for an adult at rest is 70 beats a minute. The rate for a younger person ranges from 60 to 90.

Taking the Wrist Pulse: Place the tips of your index and middle fingers on the underside of the wrist—an inch or two below the base of the thumb. Looking at the second hand of a watch or clock, count the number of pulses that occur in 60 seconds.

Practice using this method (1) to read your *own* pulse, and (2) to read the pulses of others.

Taking the Neck Pulse: Here's another method for reading your own pulse, which is often used by athletes. Place your thumb against your chin; then touch the artery on either side of your Adam's apple with the tips of your two first fingers.

A shortcut is to count the number of pulses in 10 seconds; then multiply by 6 to get the pulse rate for 60 seconds.

The School Trip

EMERGENCY #9

Brian and Carlos went with their class on a field trip to the city. They were to spend the day at the Natural History Museum.

After lunch, Brian and Carlos got bored. They decided to look for a little "adventure" on their own.

When their teacher wasn't looking, they grabbed their coats and slipped out the side door—right into the middle of the busy city.

To Brian and Carlos, the city was very exciting. The traffic noises. The tall buildings. The fancy store windows. The busy crowds rushing along the sidewalk.

"What should we do?" asked Carlos, suddenly feeling a little nervous.

Brian answered boldly, "Let's explore!"

So they walked a few blocks up the busy street that the museum was on. Then they heard fire engine sirens a few blocks away. So they ran up the street to try to spot the fire trucks.

It wasn't very long before the boys realized that they had walked quite far from the museum. They tried to find their way back.

Finally, Brian and Carlos had to admit it—they were lost.

Carlos was very worried. "What are we going to do?"

Brian knew best. "We'll just be smart. We'll retrace our steps."

They tried to find buildings that looked familiar to them. But every street corner began to look the same. Soon they found themselves even *more* lost.

Carlos spotted a taxi and waved it down. The boys asked how much it would cost to get back to the museum. Even between them, they didn't have nearly enough money!

Brian saw a newsstand that was selling maps of the city. They *did* have enough money to buy a map. But when they opened up the map, they discovered they didn't have a clue about how to read it.

Carlos was getting really scared. "How about calling the police and telling them we're lost?" he asked.

Brian answered, "No way! We're already in enough trouble as it is!"

Carlos looked at his watch. It was almost 3 o'clock—the time that their class bus was supposed to leave the museum for home.

Brian and Carlos both began to panic. Their adventure had turned into a real disaster! They had no idea what to do next.

THE SCHOOL TRIP

Activity Sheet 9

QUESTIONS TO TALK ABOUT

1. What should Brian and Carlos have done *to prevent* this emergency?

2. What mistakes did Brian and Carlos make in how they dealt with being lost? What could they have done *to handle* the situation differently?

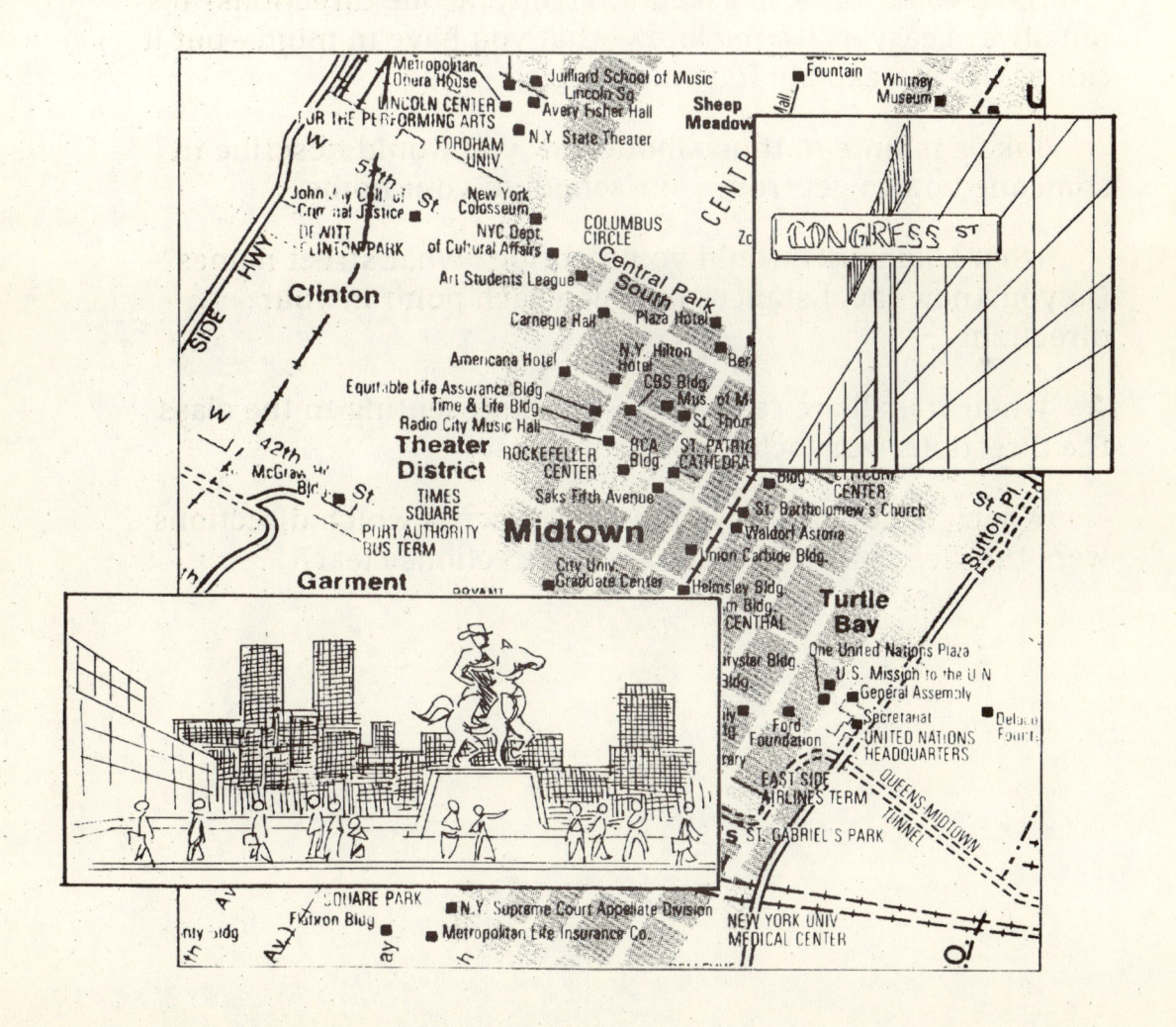

Activities to Try

1. Share Your Own Experience

Tell your class about a time when *you* were lost: Where were you? What happened? How did you get lost?

Tell how you felt.

How did the situation get solved? How would you handle the situation differently if it happened again?

2. Class Activity—Giving Directions

Have you ever been asked to give someone directions? It's not always easy, is it? *You* know what you have in mind—but it can be hard to explain to someone else.

Take a minute to think about how you would describe to someone how to get from your school to your home.

What landmarks would you mention? What street names? Do you know the distances between each point in your directions?

When you all are ready, take turns presenting to the class the directions from school to your house.

When all students have finished, discuss which directions were the clearest. What made these directions clear?

PART III. On the Road

Joy Ride

EMERGENCY #10

On his seventeenth birthday, Al bought a red pickup truck. He was very proud. He had been saving for three years.

Al's bright red truck looked almost new. It was in mint condition, with only 40,000 miles on it.

Al was so excited when he drove home from the used-car dealer. He stopped by to show his truck off to all his friends. They were as excited as Al was.

Pretty soon there was a big crowd riding with Al in his new truck. Two friends rode with Al in the front. They didn't bother to wear safety belts. Other friends rode in the open part of the truck in the back.

"Hey, Al," shouted Fred from the back. "You're the luckiest guy I know!"

As they cruised along, one friend turned up the radio full blast. Other friends waved their arms and jumped around in the back of the truck. Everyone was yelling to people they knew on the street.

"Hey," yelled Scott. "How fast can this thing go, anyway?"

"Yeah," added Don. "Let's see some speed!"

Al really liked all the attention he and his new truck were getting. "OK," he said, "Let's go down to the Strip and see!"

The Strip was a deserted road on the outskirts of town. Drivers raced their cars and trucks there—when the police weren't around.

Al and his friends arrived at the Strip. No one else was there. Everyone on the truck cheered.

Chester shouted, "Let it rip, Al!"

Al put the accelerator to the floor. The bright red truck began to gain speed.

Everybody in the back stood up and started shouting, "Faster...Faster..."

Al kept pushing the truck to go faster. Everybody was yelling louder and louder.

Then, all of a sudden, the right front tire hit a deep pothole. The speeding truck swerved off the road and rammed into a tree. There was a huge crash and splintering of glass.

Everyone in the truck was seriously injured. They were treated for broken arms, broken legs, and deep cuts all over their bodies.

Al spent the next three months in the hospital with a broken back. He never drove his new truck again. It was completely destroyed in the crash.

JOY RIDE

Activity Sheet 10

QUESTIONS TO TALK ABOUT

1. What actions could Al have taken *to prevent* this emergency?

2. What mistakes did Al make in how he dealt with his friends while he was driving? What should he have done *to handle* the situation differently?

Activities to Try

1. Make Up a Humorous "Safe Driving" Skit

Being a safe driver can be difficult. It takes a great deal of concentration. Getting distracted can be very dangerous for you.

Break up into teams to make up skits about safe driving. First, set up chairs to represent the inside of a car, van, or truck.

Choose students to play the driver and passengers. (They can be teenagers, young children, older people—any characters you choose.)

In the first skit, show all the ways that passengers can distract the driver. Be as humorous as you like. Show how things can really get out of hand.

In the second skit, show how the driver can choose to eliminate these distractions. Show what the driver can do or say to keep things safe.

2. Discussion: Talking About Accidents

Talk to your classmates about actual motor vehicle accidents—or near accidents—that *you* have been involved in, or know about.

Tell what happened. Did the behavior of the passengers contribute to the emergency?

Could the driver have acted differently in any way to prevent the accident?

Jack's Dream Date

EMERGENCY #11

Jack had it made...

He was driving his brother's fancy car. His date, Tina, was by his side.

It was the first time Jack had dated Tina. The weather report was for a clear, moonlit night. It was going to be a night to remember!

Jack and Tina were on their way to a big party in the next town. They were driving along a deserted country road. They were dressed in their finest clothes.

Suddenly, the left front tire exploded with a noise like a pistol shot! Dave pulled over.

Dave smiled at Tina. "Just a flat tire," he said. "I'll have it fixed in a minute!"

Dave grabbed in the glove compartment for the car flashlight and flicked the button. There was no light! "Batteries are dead," he said under his breath.

In the dark, he searched for the car manual to tell him how to change the tire for his brother's model of car. That was missing, too. Great!

Next, Jack opened the trunk and pulled out the spare tire. At least, that wasn't missing! In the dark he also found the jack and figured out where to attach it to the car.

The sky was clouding over. Suddenly it felt like rain. Dave knew he had to work more quickly.

In rushing back to the trunk to get the jack handle, he slipped in the muddy road. His white shirt and dress pants were now caked with mud.

Trying to control his anger, Jack looked all through the trunk, but there was no jack handle. "What more could happen?" he asked himself.

At that instant, a bolt of lightning streaked across the sky. The rain started to fall in buckets. In seconds Jack was drenched.

Jack got back into the car. He was soaking wet and covered in mud. His dream date had turned into a nightmare.

"I don't think we're going to get to that party, Tina," he said quietly. "How do you feel about hitchhiking back into town when the rain stops?"

Tina looked annoyed—while Jack swore under his breath that he would *never* borrow his brother's car again!

Jack's Dream Date 59

JACK'S DREAM DATE

Activity Sheet 11

QUESTIONS TO TALK ABOUT

1. What actions could Jack have taken *to prevent* this emergency?

2. What should Jack have done *to handle* this emergency situation differently?

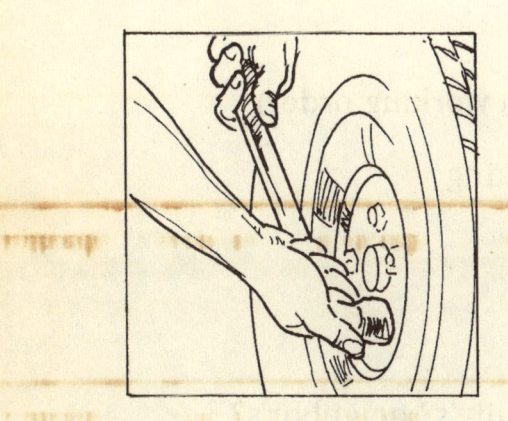

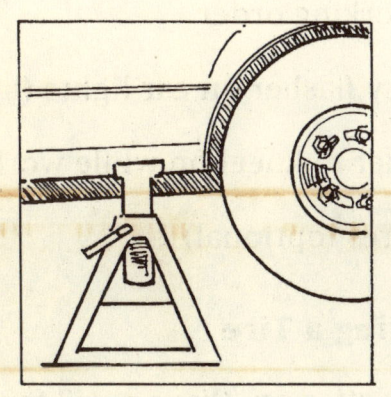

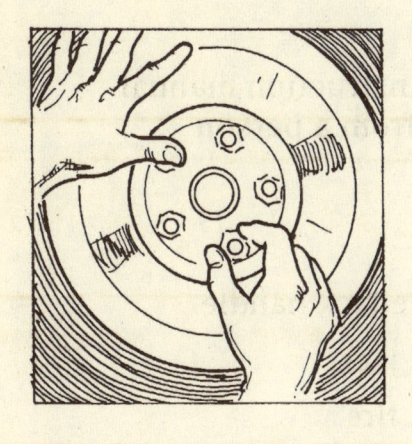

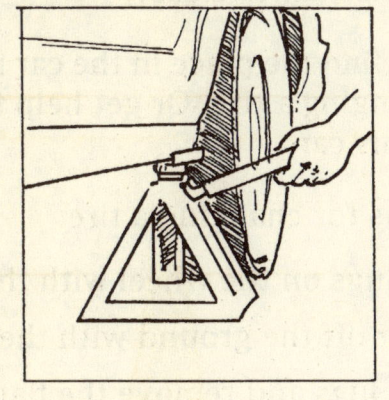

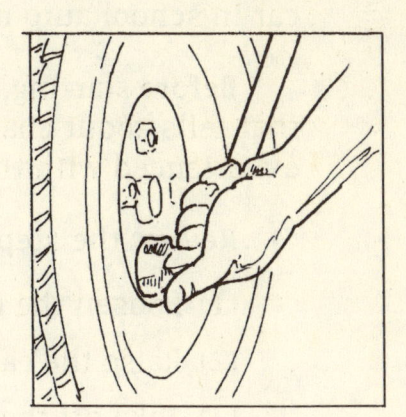

Activities to Try

1. Checklist: Be Prepared for a Flat Tire

Is the car that you drive ready for a flat tire emergency like Jack's?

Put a check mark beside each of the items below that are in the car you use.

____ Flashlight (with fresh batteries)

____ Car instruction manual

____ Spare tire (filled with correct air pressure)

____ Jack handle (that fits lug size on wheels)

____ Jack in working order

____ Emergency flasher on car lights (in working order)

____ Old blanket to kneel on while working

____ Safety flares (optional)

2. Practice Changing a Tire

Find a car to practice on. (Your own? family's? neighbor's? car in school auto mechanics class?)

Before starting, find the place in the car instruction manual that tells about changing a tire. Or get help from a person experienced with this car.

Review the steps for changing a tire:

(1) Loosen the lugs on the wheel with the jack handle.

(2) Raise the car off the ground with the jack.

(3) Take off the lugs and remove the flat tire.

(4) Put on the spare tire and loosely screw on the lugs.

(5) Lower the car to the ground.

(6) Tighten the lugs.

When you are ready, time yourself. How long does it take you to completely remove one tire and replace it with the spare tire?

Which steps gave you the most trouble? What could you do to complete these steps faster next time?

Now, try changing the spare tire back to the original tire. How much time did you save?

Full Throttle

EMERGENCY #12

Paul's parents hadn't been getting along. It seemed as if they were always fighting.

Last night Paul's father came home drunk. He yelled at Paul all through dinner.

Paul couldn't take it any longer. Without a word, he stormed out of the house and jumped on his motorcycle.

He revved the engine loudly. Then Paul roared off into the dark—without looking back.

After riding a while, Paul realized he had forgotten his helmet.

"It doesn't matter," he told himself. "Nothing matters."

It was a hot summer night. Paul was wearing a T-shirt and shorts. The warm breeze ran over his bare arms and legs.

Paul was angry and full of energy. The rush of the wind through his hair made Paul feel unbeatable.

At each stoplight in town, Paul revved his engine and looked meanly at the driver of every car. When the light turned green, he laughed and roared ahead down the road.

As Paul sped down the main street of town, he turned the throttle up, higher and higher. The bike picked up speed.

The roar of the racing motor and the feel of the bike vibrating beneath him made Paul feel like he was ruler of the world!

"I'm *never* going back!" he screamed in the wind.

Paul didn't notice the car pulling out of the side street until it was too late. It was full of drunk kids who were singing loudly and paying no attention to the road.

Their car swerved way out across the center line. Paul had no time to change direction. He was terrified.

The last thing Paul heard before the bike flipped over was the sound of laughing kids as they sped by. They had never even seen him.

FULL THROTTLE

Activity Sheet 12

QUESTIONS TO TALK ABOUT

1. What actions could Paul have taken *to prevent* this emergency?

2. What mistakes did Paul make when riding his motorcycle through town? What could he have done *to handle* the situation differently?

Activities to Try

1. Handling Emotions—On and Off the Road

Strong emotions, such as anger, are sometimes hard to handle. But they can be especially dangerous when the person feeling them is also driving a vehicle.

Paul took his angry feelings out on the road. List five safer ways for Paul to have expressed his anger (for example, going for a long walk or run, calling a friend to talk, etc.)

(1)

(2)

(3)

(4)

(5)

Think about what *you* do when *you* get angry. Share your ideas with the rest of the class. Which ways to handle strong feelings might work the best?

2. Motorcycle Safety Quiz

Riding a motorcycle can be a lot of fun. It also can be dangerous.

Put a check mark beside all the statements below that are *true* for motorcycle safety.

_____ 1. Wearing a helmet is not necessary at slow speeds.

_____ 2. Driving in the daytime is more dangerous than driving at night.

_____ 3. Motorcycles are hard for other drivers to see.

___ 4. The most serious injuries suffered in motorcycle accidents are head injuries.

___ 5. Riding a motorcycle on a rainy day is more dangerous.

___ 6. Riding a motorcycle in city traffic is easiest.

___ 7. When riding a motorcycle, it's important to ride as close as possible to the car ahead.

___ 8. Once you learn how to ride a motorcycle properly, you can relax on the road.

How many answers did you get right?

The Mountain Road

EMERGENCY #13

Donna and Stacy lived in a small town at the base of a high mountain. Near the top of the mountain was a famous ski resort.

One late October day, Donna got a call from some friends. They were having a "Goodbye Summer" party at their ski house up on the mountain.

Donna asked her friend Stacy if she wanted to drive up the mountain to the party.

"A party? Let's go!" Stacy answered. Ten minutes later, they jumped in Donna's car and were on their way.

In town, at the base of the mountain, it was 50 degrees. The sun was shining brightly and the day felt warm.

"It's going to be beautiful on top of the mountain today," said Donna. "I have a *good* feeling about this!"

But Donna was wrong. Donna and Stacy had forgotten how suddenly the weather could change up on the mountain at this time of year.

They had been driving up the mountain road for about half an hour, talking about the party all the way. Suddenly Stacy thought she saw a snowflake on the windshield.

"Is that what I think it is, Donna?" Stacy asked.

"Don't worry, Stacy. It's only a flurry," Donna answered.

Within minutes, however, the flurry turned into a real snowstorm! The snow was falling fast and thick. It was even getting hard to see the road ahead.

"Wow. This could get wild, Donna. Do you think we should head back?"

"Nah. I drive in this kind of stuff all the time. We'll be fine," said Donna confidently.

"Well, I'm glad your brother made that appointment to get the snow tires on last week."

For a moment, Donna didn't say a word. Then she spoke.

"I hate to tell you this, Stacy, but Tim had to go to the doctor last Wednesday. He never got the tires changed."

Suddenly the car began to swerve back and forth on the mountain road. At one moment it looked as if the car might even slide off the road and over the cliff.

"We're going to die!" screamed Stacy.

But then the car skidded in the other direction and rolled down into a ditch.

Luckily the girls weren't injured. But Donna and Stacy never made it to the party.

A passing car reported the accident. Two hours later a tow truck came to take Donna's car down the mountain.

THE MOUNTAIN ROAD

Activity Sheet 13

QUESTIONS TO TALK ABOUT

1. What actions should Donna and Stacy have taken *to prevent* this emergency?

2. What mistakes did Donna and Stacy make in how they dealt with having to drive in the snow? What could they have done *to handle* the situation differently?

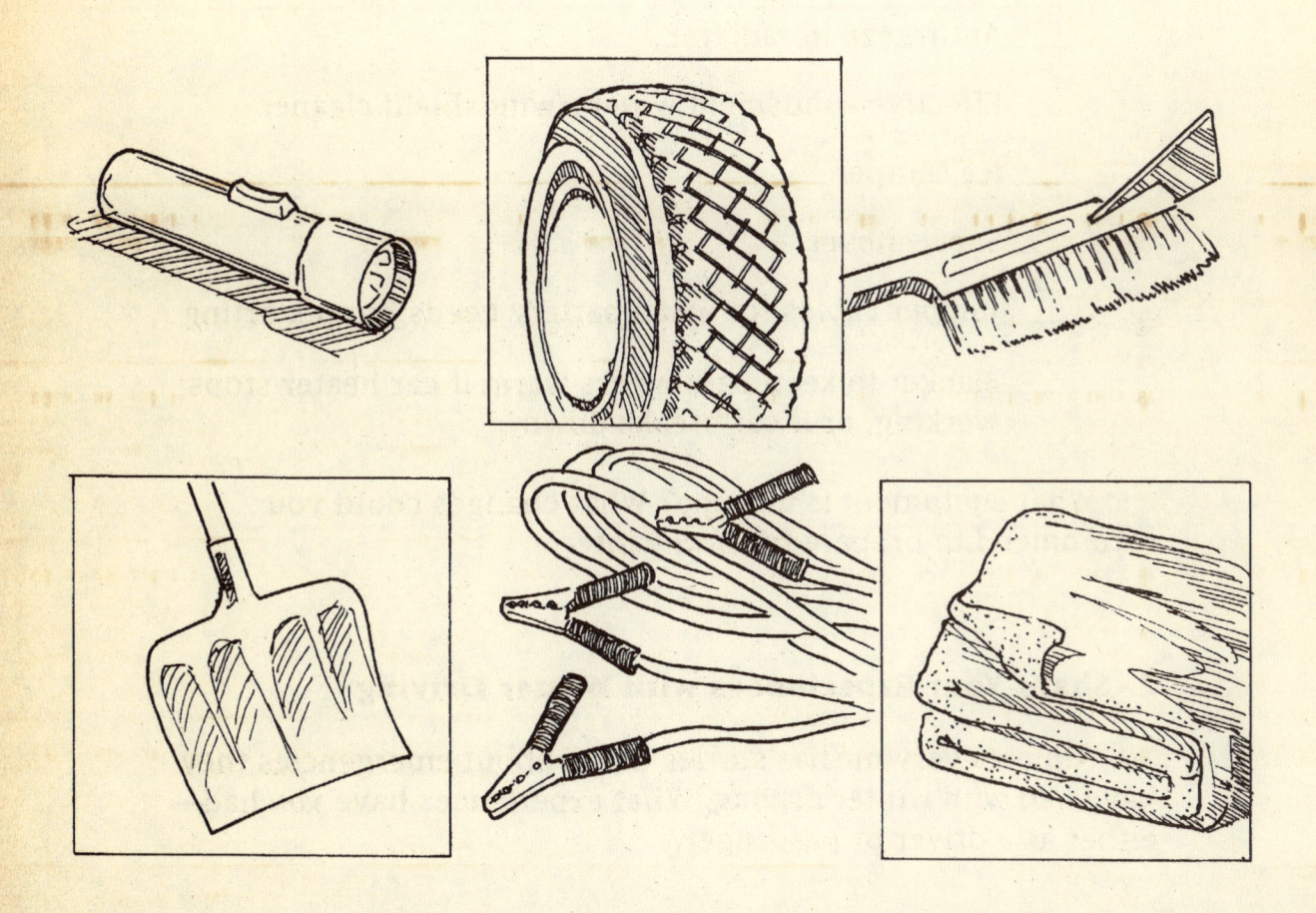

Activities to Try

1. Checklist for Getting a Car Ready for Winter Weather

Every car needs to be specially prepared and equipped for winter weather.

Think about the car you drive. (Your own car? your family's car? a friend's or relative's car?) How well is it equipped for winter driving each year?

Put a check mark by each of the items below that are regularly included in preparing your car for winter.

____ Flashlight (in working order)

____ Snow tires (or chains)

____ Antifreeze in radiator

____ Effective windshield wipers/windshield cleaner

____ Ice scraper

____ Snow shovel

____ Jumper cables for when battery needs jump-starting

____ Blanket to keep passengers warm if car heater stops working, or if car breaks down

What equipment is missing? What changes could you recommend to prepare for *next* winter?

2. Share Your Experiences with Winter Driving

Almost everyone has stories to tell about emergencies they have had with winter driving. What experiences have *you* had—either as a driver or passenger?

Have you ever been caught in a sudden storm like Donna and Stacy? Have you ever had to drive in snow without snow tires or chains?

Share your experiences with other members of your class.

Hit and Run

EMERGENCY #14

Tom's mother had a problem. She was in the middle of making a birthday cake when she ran out of eggs.

Tom and his friend Don were watching a basketball play-off on television in the other room. Tom's mother sent them to the store to buy eggs.

"Why did she have to run out of eggs now?" Tom moaned. "The score was tied in the last quarter!"

"Drive faster!" urged Don. "Maybe we can get back in time to see the end of the game."

Tom's mind was definitely not on driving. All he could think about was the game they were missing.

Suddenly, Don felt the left front wheel hit something with a loud thump. Tom kept right on driving.

"Didn't you feel that, Tom?" asked Don.

"What?" answered Tom.

"I think we hit something."

"Aw, forget it," Tom said. "We need to get to the store."

But Don's conscience was bothering him.

"Tom, really, I think we should go back. I think we hit something."

Muttering under his breath, Tom turned the car around and retraced their route.

There in the middle of the other lane was a small furry dog. It was lying completely still.

"What'll we do now?" Tom said nervously. "It looks dead."

"I'm going to get it out of the road," said Don. He got out of the car and walked over to the animal.

"I think it *is* dead," he yelled as he began to pull it by the front legs.

Suddenly the dog began to growl viciously. Then the dog bared his teeth and bit Don's hand.

The boys never made it back to watch the end of the basketball game.

Tom spent the next two hours knocking on doors to find the owner of the dog he had hit. And Don had to be rushed to the hospital for rabies shots.

HIT AND RUN

Activity Sheet 14

QUESTIONS TO TALK ABOUT

1. What actions could Tom and Don have taken *to prevent* this emergency?

2. What mistakes did Tom and Don make in how they dealt with hitting the dog? What should they have done *to handle* the situation differently?

Activities to Try

1. Tell About Your Experience

Have *you* ever been in a car accident involving an animal? What happened?

What kind of animal was hit? Whose fault was the accident?

Could the accident have been prevented? Tell how.

What happened after the animal was hit? Was the animal injured or killed? Did someone have to move or handle the dog?

Would you recommend acting differently in any way if a similar situation happened today?

2. Find Out the Best Way to Handle a Hurt Animal

There are many do's and don'ts about how to handle an injured animal.

First, make a list of questions that your class would like to have answered. (For example, "How do you know if the animal is still alive?" "Should you try to move it?" etc.)

Then, invite an expert from your town, such as a veterinarian, game warden, or police officer, to visit your class. What information can this expert give you to answer your questions?